Charles Chaucer Goss

Hymns Adapted to Christians of Every Name

Charles Chaucer Goss

Hymns Adapted to Christians of Every Name

ISBN/EAN: 9783744779449

Printed in Europe, USA, Canada, Australia, Japan

Cover: Foto ©Lupo / pixelio.de

More available books at **www.hansebooks.com**

ADAPTED TO

Christians of Every Name.

Rev.———

BY CHARLES CHAUCER GOSS.

∧ ———

.

NEW-YORK

EVANGELICAL ALLIANCE.

NEW-YORK.

1861.

Printed and Stereotyped by
SACKETT & COBB,
25 John Street, New-York.

Jesus Christ.

.1.   C M.

ALL hail the power of Jesus' name.
   Let angels prostrate fall;
Bring forth the royal diadem,
   And crown him Lord of all.

Ye saints redeemed of Adam's race,
   Ye ransomed from the fall,
Hail him who saves you by his grace!
   And crown him Lord of all.

Let every kindred, every tribe
   On this terrestrial ball,
To him all majesty ascribe,
   And crown him Lord of all.

O that with yonder sacred throng
   We at his feet may fall,
Join in the everlasting song,
   And crown him Lord of all.

2.   8s & 7s.

HARK!—what mean those holy voices,
    Sweetly sounding through the skies?
Lo! the angelic host rejoices;
    Heavenly hallelujahs rise.
Hear them tell the wondrous story,
    Hear them chant, in hymns of joy,
" Glory in the highest—glory!
    Glory be to God most high!"

Peace on earth—good will from heaven,
    Reaching far as man is found.
" Souls redeem'd, and sins forgiven,"
    Loud our golden harps shall sound.
Christ is born, the great Anointed;
    Heaven and earth his praises sing!
Oh, receive whom God appointed
    For your Prophet, Priest and King,

3.   8s 7s & 4s.

ANGELS, from the realms of glory,
    Wing your flight o'er all the earth,
Ye who sang creation's story,
    Now proclaim Messiah's birth;
        Come and worship,
Worship Christ the new-born King.

Shepherds, in the field abiding,
    Watching o'er your flocks by night,
God with man is now residing,
    Yonder shines the infant-light;
        Come and worship,
Worship Christ the new-born King.

Sages, leave your contemplations,
 Brighter visions beam afar;
Seek the great Desire of nations;
 Ye have seen his natal star;
  Come and worship,
Worship Christ the new-born King.

Saints, before the altar bending,
 Watching long in hope and fear,
Suddenly, the Lord descending,
 In his temple shall appear;
  Come and worship,
Worship Christ, the new-born King.

4. S. M.

FATHER, our hearts we lift
 Up to thy gracious throne,
And thank thee for the precious gift
 Of thine incarnate Son.

The gift unspeakable
 We thankfully receive,
And to the world thy goodness tell,
 And to thy glory live.

May all mankind receive
 The new-born Prince of peace.
And meekly in his spirit live,
 And in his love increase.

Till he convey us home,
 Cry every soul aloud,—
Come, thou Desire of nations, come,
 And take us up to God.

5.   C. M.

PLUNGED in a gulf of dark despair
　We wretched sinners lay,
Without one cheering beam of hope,
　Or spark of glimmering day.

With pitying eyes the Prince of peace
　Beheld our helpless grief;
He saw, and (O amazingly lone!)
　He flew to our relief.

Down from the shining seats above,
　With joyful haste he fled;
Entered the grave in mortal flesh,
　And dwelt among the dead.

O for this love let rocks and hills
　Their lasting silence break;
And all harmonious human tongues,
　The Saviour's praises speak.

Angels, assist our mighty joys;
　Strike all your harps of gold;
But when you raise your highest notes
　His love can ne'er be told.

6.   7s.

GOD *with us!* O glorious name
　Let it shine in endless fame.
God and man in Christ unite;
O mysterious depth and height!

God *with us!* th' eternal Son
Took our souls, our flesh, and bone,
Now, ye saints, his grace admire,
Swell the song with holy fire.

God *with us!* but tainted not
With the first transgressor's blot ;
Yet he did our sins sustain,
Bear the guilt, the curse, the pain.

God *with us!* O wondrous grace.
Let us see him face to face ;
That we may *Immanuel* sing,
As we ought, our God and King.

7.   C. M.

ALAS! and did my Saviour bleed ?
And did my Sovereign die ?
Would he devote that sacred head
For such a worm as I ?

Was it for crimes that I had done
He groan'd upon the tree ?
Amazing pity ! grace unknown
And love beyond degree !

Well might the sun in darkness hide,
And shut his glories in,
When Christ the bless'd Redeemer died
For man, the creature's sin.

Thus might I hide my blushing face
While his dear cross appears,·
Dissolve my heart in thankfulness,
And melt mine eyes to tears.

But drops of grief can ne'er repay
The debt of love I owe :
Here, Lord, I give myself away ;
'Tis all that I can do.

8. L. M.

WHEN I survey the wondrous cross,
  On which the Prince of glory died;
My richest gain I count but loss,
  And pour contempt on all my pride.

Forbid it, Lord, that I should boast,
  Save in the death of Christ, my God;
All the vain things that charm me most,
  I sacrifice them to his blood.

See, from his head, his hands, his feet,
  Sorrow and love flow mingled down;
Did e'er such love and sorrow meet,
  Or thorns compose so rich a crown!

Were the whole realm of nature mine
  That were a present far too small;
Love so amazing, so divine,
  Demands my soul, my life, my all.

9. L, M.

'TIS finished! so the Saviour cried,
  And meekly bowed his head and died;
'Tis finished! yes, the race is run,
The battle fought, the victory won.

'Tis finished! let the joyful sound
Be heard through all the nations round;
'Tis finished! let the echo fly,
Through heaven and hell, through earth and sky.

10.   C. L. M.

HOW calm and beautiful the morn,
　　That gilds the sacred tomb,
Where once the Crucified was borne,
　　And veil'd in midnight gloom!
O, weep no more the Saviour slain;
The Lord is risen—he lives again.

How tranquil now the rising day,
　　'Tis Jesus still appears,
A risen Lord to chase away
　　Your unbelieving fears:
O, weep no more your comforts slain,
The Lord is risen—he lives again.

And when the shades of evening fall,
　　When life's last hour draws nigh,
If Jesus shines upon the soul,
　　How blissful then to die;
Since he has risen who once was slain,
Ye die in Christ to live again.

11.   L. M.

I KNOW that my Redeemer lives;
　What comfort this sweet sentence gives
He lives, he lives, who once was dead,
He lives, my ever-living head.

He lives to bless me with his love,
He lives to plead for me above,
He lives my hungry soul to feed,
He lives to help in time of need.

He lives to silence all my fears,
He lives to wipe away my tears,
He lives to calm my troubled heart,
He lives, all blessings to impart.

He lives, all glory to his name!
He lives, my Jesus, still the same;
O the sweet joy this sentence gives,
I know that my Redeemer lives!

12.   C. M.

THE head that once was crown'd with thorns,
  Is crown'd with glory now;
A royal diadem adorns
  The mighty Victor's brow.

The highest place that heaven affords,
  Is to our Jesus given;
The King of kings, and Lord of lords,
  He reigns o'er earth and heaven.

13.   C. M.

COME, let us join our cheerful songs
  With angels round the throne;
Ten thousand thousand are their tongues,
  But all their joys are one.

" Worthy the Lamb that died," they cry,
  " To be exalted thus:"
" Worthy the Lamb," our lips reply,
  " For he was slain for us."

Jesus is worthy to receive
  Honor and power divine;
And blessings more than we can give,
  Be, Lord, for ever thine.

14. C. P. M.

O, COULD we speak the matchless worth,
  O, could we sound the glories forth,
    Which in our Saviour shine,
We'd soar, and touch the heavenly strings,
And vie with Gabriel, when he sings,
    In notes almost divine.

We'd sing the characters he bears,
And all the forms of love he wears,
    Exalted on his throne;
In loftiest songs of sweetest praise,
We would to everlasting days,
    Make all his glories known.

Soon the delightful day will come,
When Christ, our Lord, will bring us home
    And we shall see his face;
Then with our Saviour, Brother, Friend,
A blest eternity we'll spend
    Triumphant in his grace.

15. C. M.

HOW sweet the name of Jesus sounds
  In a believer's ear!
It soothes his sorrows, heals his wounds,
  And drives away his fear.

It makes the wounded spirit whole,
  And calms the troubled breast;
'Tis manna to the hungry soul,
  And to the weary rest.

JESUS CHRIST.

I would thy boundless love proclaim,
  With every fleeting breath;
And may the music of thy name
  Refresh my soul in death.

CHORUS.

I do believe, I now believe,
  That Jesus died for me,
And through his blood, his precious blood,
  I shall from sin be free.

16.   H. M.

LET earth and heaven agree
  Angels and men be joined,
To celebrate with me
  The Saviour of mankind:
To' adore the all-atoning Lamb,
And bless the sound of Jesus' name.

Jesus! transporting name!
  It charms the hosts above;
They evermore proclaim,
  And wonder at his love:
'Tis all their happiness to gaze,—
'Tis heaven to see our Jesus' face.

His name the sinner hears,
  And is from sin set free;
'Tis music in his ears;
  'Tis life and victory;
New songs do now his lips employ,
And dances his glad heart for joy.

17.   H. M.

JOIN all the glorious names
 Of wisdom, love and pow'r,
That ever mortals knew,
That angels ever bore;
All are too mean to speak his worth;
Too mean to set my Saviour forth.

Jesus, my great *High Priest*,
Offered his blood, and died;
My guilty conscience seeks
No sacrifice beside.
His precious blood did once atone;
And now it pleads before the throne.

My dear and mighty Lord,
My Conqu'ror, and my *King*,
Thy sceptre and thy sword,
Thy reigning grace I sing.
I shall be safe, for Christ displays
Superior pow'r and guardian grace.

18.   L. .M.

AWAKE, my soul, to joyful lays,
 And sing the great Redeemer's praise;
He justly claims a song from me,
His loving-kindness, Oh, how free!

He saw me ruin'd in the fall,
Yet loved me notwithstanding all:
He sav'd me from my lost estate,
His loving-kindness, Oh, how great!

When trouble, like a gloomy cloud,
Has gather'd thick, and thunder'd loud.
He near my soul has always stood,
His loving-kindness, Oh, how good!

Soon shall I pass the gloomy vale,
Soon all my mortal pow'rs must fail;
Oh! may my last expiring breath
His loving-kindness sing in death!

19.   8s. & 7s.

HARK! ten thousand harps and voices
    Sound the notes of praise above;
Jesus reigns, and heaven rejoices:
    Jesus reigns, the God of love.
See, He sits on yonder throne!
Jesus rules the world alone.
    Hallelujah! hallelujah! hallelujah! Amen!

King of glory, reign forever,
    Thine an everlasting crown;
Nohting from thy love shall sever
    Those whom thou has made thine own—
Happy objects of thy grace,
Destined to behold thy face.
    Hallelujah! hallelujah! hallelujah! Amen!

The Gospel of Christ.

THE gospel! O, what endless charms
 Dwell in that blissful sound;
Its influence every fear disarms,
 And spreads delight around.

Here pardon, life and joy divine,
 In rich effusion flow,
For guilty rebels, lost in sin,
 And doom'd to endless woe.

How rich the depths of love divine!
 Of bliss, a boundless store!
Redeemer, let me call thee mine,—
 Thy fulness I implore.

On thee alone my hope relies;
 Beneath thy cross I fall;
My Lord, my life, my sacrifice,
 My Saviour, and my all.

21.   L. M.

GO, preach my gospel, saith the Lord,—
    Bid the whole earth my grace receive;
He shall be saved who trusts my word,
    And he condemned who won't believe.

I'll make your great commission known;
    And ye shall prove my gospel true,
By all the works that I have done,
    By all the wonders ye shall do.

Teach all the nations my commands,—
    I'm with you till the world shall end;
All powers is trusted in my hands,—
    I can destroy and I defend.

22.   7s.

ROCK of Ages! cleft for me,
    Let me hide myself in thee;
Let the water and the blood
From thy wounded side that flowed,
Be of sin the perfect cure,
Save from wrath, and make me pure.

Should my tears forever flow,
Should my zeal no languor know,
This for sin could not atone—
Thou must save, and thou alone.
In my hand no price I bring;
Simply to thy cross I cling.

While I draw this fleeting breath,
When mine eyelids close in death,
When I rise to worlds unknown,
And behold thee on thy throne,
Rock of Ages! cleft for me,
Let me hide myself in thee,

23.   C. M.

O WHAT amusing words of grace
   Are in the gospel found;
Suited to every sinner's case
   Who hears the joyful sound.

Come, then, with all your wants and wounds,
   Your every burden bring;
Here love, unchanging love, abounds,
   A deep celestial spring.

Millions of sinners vile as you,
   Have here found life and peace;
Come, then, and prove its virtues too,
   And drink, adore and bless.

24.   L. M.

JUST as I am, without one plea,
   But that thy blood was shed for me,
And that thou bidd'st me come to thee,
      O Lamb of God, I come!

Just as I am, though tossed about
With many a conflict, many a doubt,
With fears within and wars without,
      O Lamb of God, I come!

Just as I am, poor, wretched, blind,
Sight, riches, healing of the mind,
Yea, all I need, in thee to find,
      O Lamb of God, I come!

Just as I am—thou wilt receive,
Wilt welcome, pardon, cleanse, relieve,
Because thy promise I believe—
      O Lamb of God, I come!

Just as I am—Thy love unknown
Has broken every barrier down;
Now to be thine, yea, thine alone—
O Lamb of God, I come!

25.   8s 7s & 4s.

COME, ye sinners, poor and needy,
  Weak and wounded, sick and sore;
Jesus ready stands to save you,
  Full of mercy, love, and power.
      He is able,
He is willing: doubt no more.

Ho! ye needy, come and welcome,
  God's free bounty glorify;
True belief, and true repentance,
  Every grace that brings us nigh.
      Without money
Come to Jesus Christ, and buy.

Let not conscience make you linger,
  Nor of fitness fondly dream!
All the fitness he requireth,
  Is to feel your need of him.
      This he gives you,
'Tis the spirit's rising beam.

Lo! th' incarnate God ascended,
  Pleads the merit of his blood,
Venture on him, venture wholly,
  Let no other trust intrude;
      None but Jesus
Can do helpless sinners good.

26.   S. M.

WHAT majesty and grace
  Through all the gospel shine!
'Tis God that speaks, and we confess
  The doctrine most divine.

Down from his throne on high,
  The mighty Saviour comes;
Lays his bright robes of glory by,
  And feeble flesh assumes.

The debt that sinners owed
  Upon the cross he pays;
Then through the clouds ascends to God,
  'Midst shouts of loftiest praise.

There our High Priest appears,
  Before his Father's throne,
Mingles his merits with our tears,
  And pours salvation down.

27   8s & 7s.

LOVE divine, all love excelling!
  Joy of heav'n, to earth come down!
Fix in us thy humble dwelling;
  All thy faithful mercies crown.

Jesus, thou art all compassion!
  Pure, unbounded love, thou art!
Visit us with thy salvation,
  Enter ev'ry trembling heart.

Breathe, O breathe, thy loving Spirit
  Into ev'ry troubled breast!
Let us all in thee inherit,
  Let us find thy promis'd rest.

Chang'd from glory unto glory,
  Till in heaven we take our place;
Till we cast our crowns before thee,
  Lost in wonder, love and praise!

28. C. M.

SALVATION! O, the joyful sound;
  'Tis pleasure to our ears;
A sov'reign balm for every wound,
  A cordial for our fears.

Salvation! let the echo fly
  The spacious earth around,
While all the armies of the sky
  Conspire to raise the sound.

Salvation! Oh thou bleeding Lamb,
  To thee the praise belongs:
Salvation shall inspire our hearts,
  And dwell upon our tongues.

CHORUS.

Glory, honor, praise and power,
Be unto the Lamb forever!
Jesus Christ is our Redeemer!
Hallelujah, praise the Lord!

29. 11s & 10s.

SOUND the full chorus! let praises ascend
  To God our Redeemer, our Saviour, and
    Friend.
Sing! for the light of his truth is before us,
And we will give thanks and rejoice in his name;
His banner of love in its glory waves o'er us;
That love will continue forever the same.
      Sound the full chorus, &c.

Praise to our Jesus! Give praise—let it rise
From earth, in its fulness, and swell to the skies!
  Give glory and praise! For a ransomed crea-
    tion
The gospel of peace in its triumph shall see;
  Jesus hath redeemed us, and He our salva-
    tion,
Appears from transgression and death to make
    free!
          Praise to our Jesus, &c.

30.   7s.

HASTEN, Lord, the glorious time,
  When, beneath Messiah's sway,
Every nation, every clime,
  Shall the gospel call obey!

Mightiest kings his power shall own,
  Heathen tribes his name adore;
Satan and his host, o'erthrown,
  Bound in chains shall hurt no more.

Then shall wars and tumults cease,
  Then be banish'd grief and pain;
Righteousness and joy and peace
  Undisturb'd shall ever reign!

Bless me, then, our gracious Lord;
  Ever praise his glorious name;
All his mighty acts record.—
  All his wondrous love proclaim.

31. L. M.

JESUS shall reign wher'er the sun
  Does his successive journeys run ;
His kingdom stretch from shore to shore,
Till suns shall rise and set no more.

For him shall endless prayer be made,
And endless praises crown his head ;
His name, like sweet perfume, shall rise
With every morning sacrifice.

People and realms of every tongue
Dwell on his love with sweetest song ;
And infant voices shall proclaim
Their early blessings on his name.

Let every creature rise and bring
Peculiar honors to our King ;
Angels descend with songs again,
And earth repeat the loud amen.

Example of Christ.

---

32.   C. M.

BEHOLD, where, in a mortal form
   Appears each grace divine;
The virtues, all in Jesus met,
   With mildest radiance shine.

To spread the rays of heavenly light,
   To give the mourner joy,
To preach good tidings to the poor,
   Was his divine employ.

'Midst keen reproach, and cruel scorn,
   Patient and meek he stood;
His foes, ungrateful, sought his life;
   He labored for their good.

Be Christ our pattern and our guide;
   His image may we bear;
O, may we tread his holy steps,
   His joy and glory share!

33. C. M.

FATHER of mercies send thy grace,
　All pow'rful, from above,
To form, in our obedient souls,
　The image of thy love.

O may our sympathizing breasts
　The generous pleasure know,
Kindly to share in others' joy,
　And weep for others' woe!

When poor and helpless sons of grief
　In deep distress are laid;
Soft be our hearts, their pains to feel,
　And swift our hands to aid.

So Jesus look'd on dying man,
　When thron'd above the skies;
And, 'midst th' embraces of his God,
　He felt compassion rise.

On wings of love the Saviour flew,
　To bless a ruined race;
We would, O Lord, thy steps pursue,
　Thy bright example trace.

34. 7s.

LORD, what offering shall we bring,
　At thine altars when we bow?
Hearts, the pure unsullied spring
　Whence the kind affection flow;
Soft compassion's feeling soul,
　By the melting eye expressed;
Sympathy, at whose control
　Sorrow leaves the wounded breast.

Willing hands to lead the blind,
  Bind the wounded, feed the poor;
Love, embracing all our kind;
  Charity, with liberal store;—
Teach us, O thou Heavenly King,
  Thus to show our grateful mind,
Thus the accepted offering bring,
  Love to thee and all mankind.

35. C. M.

GO to the home of disease,
  Where might gives no repose,
And on the cheek where sickness preys,
  Bid health to plant the rose.

Go where the friendless stranger lies,
  To perish in his gloom;
Let smiles of love fall on his eyes,
  While he's away from home.

Thus what our Heavenly Father gave
  Shall we as freely give;
And copy him who lived to save,
  And died that we might live.

36. C. M.

THINK gently of the erring one!
  O, let us not forget,
However darkly stained by sin,
  He is our brother yet!

Heir of the same inheritance,
  Child of the self-same God,
He hath but stumbled in the path
  We have in weakness trod.

Speak gently to the erring ones !
  We may yet lead them back,
With holy words, and tones of love,
  From misery's thorny track.

Forget not, brother, thou hast sinned,
  And sinful yet may'st be ;
Deal gently with the erring heart,
  As God hath dealt with thee.

37. S. M.

LABORERS of Christ arise,
  And gird you for the toil,
The dew of promise from the skies
  Already cheers the soil

Go where the sick recline,
  Where mourning hearts deplore ;
And, where the sons of sorrow pine,
  Dispense your hallowed love.

Urge with a tender zeal,
  The erring ones along,
And lead them to the feet of Christ,
  Who will forgive their wrong.

38. 7s & 6s.

WE ought to be like Jesus,
  So lowly and so meek ;
For no one marked an angry word
  That ever heard him speak.

We ought to be like Jesus,
  So frequently in prayer;
Alone upon the mountain top
  He met his Father there.

We ought to be like Jesus,
  Engaged in doing good,
So that of us it may be said:
  " She hath done what she could."

Alas! we're not like Jesus,
  As any one may see;
O, Gentle Saviour, send thy grace,
  And make us all like thee.

39.   C. M.

THY neighbor? 'tis the fainting poor
  Whose eye with want is dim;
Whose hunger sends from door to door,
  Go thou and succor him.

Thy neighbor? 'tis that weary man
  Whose years are at the brim,
Who's low with sickness, cares and pain;
  Go thou and comfort him.

Thy neighbor? 'tis the heart bereft
  Of every earthly gem;
Widow and orphan, helpless left,
  Go thou and shelter them.

Where'er thou meet'st a human form,
  Less favored than thy own,
Remmeber, 'tis thy neighbor warm,
  Live thou, or die for him.

40.   6s & 4s.

KIND words can never die :
    Heaven gave them birth ;
Wing'd with a smile, they fly
    All o'er the earth.
Kind words the angels brought,
Kind words our Saviour taught,—
Sweet melodies of thought !
    Who knows their worth ?
Kind words can never die, &c.

Kind deeds can never die :
    Though weak and small,
From his bright throne on high
    God sees them all ;
He doth reward with love
All those who faithful prove ;
Round them, where'er they move,
    Rich blessings fall.
Kind deeds can never die, &c.

41.   L. M.

BLEST is the man, whose heart is kind,
    And melts in pity to the poor ;
Who, with a sympathizing mind,
    Feels what his fellow-men endure.

His heart contrives for their relief,
    More good than his own hands can do ;
He in the time of general grief,
    Shall find the Lord hath pity too.

Or if with mortal sufferings tried,
    Sufferings shall all his soul refine ;
Sweet hope his refuge shall provide,
    And minister a bliss divine.

42.   S. M.

DID Christ o'er sinners weep?
　　And shall our cheeks be dry?
Let floods of penitential grief
　　Burst forth from every eye.

The Son of God in tears,
　　Angels with wonder see!
Be thou astonish'd, O my soul,
　　He shed those tears for thee.

He wept, that we might weep;
　　Each sin demands a tear:
In heav'n alone no sin is found,
　　And there's no weeping there.

43.   6s & 5s.

BE kind to each other!
　　The night's coming on,
When friend and when brother
　　Perchance may be gone;
Then, 'midst our dejection,
　　How sweet to have earn'd
The blest recollection
　　Of kindness return'd.

Nor change with to-morrow
　　Should fortune take wing;
The deeper the sorrow,
　　The closer still cling!
Be kind to each other!
　　The night's coming on,
When friend and when brother
　　Perchance may be gone.

EXAMPLE.

44.   C. M.

HOW condescending and how kind
  Was God's eternal Son!
Our misery reached his heavenly mind,
  And pity brought him down.

He sunk beneath our heavy woes,
  To raise us to his throne;
There's ne'er a gift his hand bestows
  But cost his heart a groan.

This was compassion like a God,
  That when the Saviour knew
The price of pardon was his blood,
  His pity ne'er withdrew.

Now, though he reigns exhalted high,
  His love is still as great;
Well he remembers Calvary,
  Nor let his saints forget.

45.   7s & 6s.

SHALL we, whose souls are lighted
  With light from Christ on high,
Shall we to men benighted,
  The lamp of truth deny?

Salvation! O Salvation!
  The joyful sound proclaim,
'Till every land and nation
  Has learned Messiah's name.

Comfort in Christ.

---

46.   L. M.

WHEN marshalled on the nightly plain,
  The glittering host bestud the sky,
One star alone, of all the train,
  Can fix the sinner's wandering eye.

Hark! hark! to God the chorus breaks,
  From every host, from every gem;
But one alone the Saviour speaks—
  It is the star of Bethlehem.

Once on the raging seas I rode:
  The storm was loud, the night was dark;
The ocean yawned, and rudely blowed
  The wind that tossed my foundering bark.

Deep horror then my vitals froze;
  Death-struck, I ceased the tide to stem;
When suddenly a star arose—
  It was the star of Bethlehem.

It was my guide, my light, my all;
   It bade my dark forebodings cease;
And through the storm and danger's thrall,
   It led me to the port of peace.

Now safely moored, my perils o'er,
   I'll sing first in night's diadem,
Forever and forevermore,
   The star—the star of Bethlehem.

47.   P. M.

BEGONE, unbelief!
   My Saviour is near;
And for my relief
   Will surely appear:
By prayer let me wrestle,
   And he will perform;
With Christ in the vessel,
   I smile at the storm.

Tho' dark be my way,
   Since 'ie is my guide,
'Tis mine to obey,
   'Tis his to provide:
His way was much rougher,
   And darker than mine;
Did Jesus thus suffer,
   And shall I repine?

His love in time past,
   Forbids me to think
He'll leave me at last
   In trouble to sink:
Tho' painful at present,
   'Twill cease before long,
And then, O how pleasant
   The conqueror's song.

48.   C. M.

JESUS, from whom all goodness flows,
  I lift my soul to thee;
In all my sorrows, conflicts, woes,
  Jesus remember me.

If for thy sake, upon my name
  Reproach and shame shall be,
I'll hail reproach, and welcome shame;
  Jesus remember me.

When worn with pain, disease, and grief,
  This feeble body be;
Grant patience, rest, and kind relief;
  Jesus remember me.

49.   P. M.

HOW happy are they
  Who the Saviour obey,
And have laid up their treasure above?
  Oh, what tongue can express
  The sweet comfort and peace
Of a soul in its earliest love?

'Twas heaven below
  My Redeemer to know,
And the angels could do nothing more
  Than to fall at his feet,
  And the story repeat,
And the lover of sinners adore.

Then all the day long,
  Was my Jesus my song,
And redemption thro' faith in his name,
  Oh, that all might believe,
  And salvation receive,
And their song and their joy be the same.

50.   L. M.

GOD of my life, whose gracious power
  Through varied depths my soul hath led,
Has shone upon the darkened hour,
  Has lifted up my sinking head.

In all my ways thy hand I own,
  Thy ruling providence I see;
Assist me still my course to run,
  And still direct my paths to thee.

Whither, O whither should I fly,
  But to my loving Saviour's breast!
Secure within his arms to lie,
  And safe beneath his wings to rest.

51.   8s & 7s

JESUS, I my cross have taken,
  All to leave, and follow thee,
Naked, poor, despised, forsaken,
  Thou from hence my all shalt be.
Perish ev'ry fond ambition,
  All I've sought, or hoped, or known;
Yet how rich is my condition!
  Christ, and heaven, are still my own.

Let the world despise, and leave me;
  They have left my Saviour too;
Human hearts and looks deceive me,
  Thou art not like them untrue;
And whilst thou shall smile upon me,
  God of wisdom, love, and might,
Foes may hate, and friends disown me,
  Show thy face, and all is bright.

52.   S. M.

GIVE to the winds thy fears,
  Hope, and be undismay'd;
Christ hears thy sighs, and counts thy tears,
  He shall lift up thy head

Through waves, and clouds, and storms,
  He gently clears thy way:
Wait thou his time; so shall this night
  Soon end in joyous day.

Still heavy is thy heart?
  Still sink thy spirits down?
Cast off the weight, let fear depart,
  And every care be gone.

What though thou rulest not?
  Yet heaven, and earth, and hell
Proclaim Christ sitteth on the throne,
  And doeth all things well.

53.   11s.

HOW firm a foundation, ye saints of the Lord,
  Is laid for your faith in his excellent word!
What more can he say than to you he hath said,
Who unto the Saviour for refuge hath fled!

" Fear not, I am with thee, O be not dismay'd,
For I am thy God, and will still give thee aid;
I'll strengthen thee, help thee, and cause thee to
      stand,
Upheld by my righteous, Omnipotent hand.

When thro' the deep waters I call thee to go,
The rivers of sorrow shall not overflow;
For I will be with thee thy troubles to bless,
And sanctify to thee thy deepest distress.

When thro' fiery trials thy pathway shall lie,
My grace all-sufficient shall be thy supply;
The flame shall not hurt thee, I only design
Thy dross to consume, and thy gold to refine.

The soul that on Jesus hath lean'd for repose,
He will not, he will not desert to his foes;
That soul, tho' all hell should endeavor to shake,
He'll never—no, never—no, never forsake."

54.   7s & 6s.

RISE, my soul, and stretch thy wings,
    Thy better portion trace;
Rise from transitory things
    Towards heaven, thy native place;
Sun, and moon, and stars decay,
    Time shall soon this earth remove;
Rise, my soul, and haste away
    To seats prepared above.

Rivers to the ocean run,
    Nor stay in all their course;
Fire, ascending, seeks the sun,
    Both speed them to their source:
So the soul that's born of God
    Pants to see his Saviour's face,
Upward tends to his abode,
    To rest in his embrace.

55. C. M.

O THOU who driest the mourner's tear,
How dark this world would be,
If, when deceived and wounded here,
We could not fly to thee.

The friends who in our sunshine live,
When Winter comes, are flown ;
And he who has but tears to give,
Must weep those tears alone.

But Christ can heal the broken heart,
Which, like the plants that throw
Their fragrance from the wounded part,
Breathes sweetness out of woe.

56. C. M.

WHILE thee I seek, protecting power,
Be my vain wishes stilled ;
And may this consecrated hour
With better hopes be filled !

In each event of life, how clear
Thy ruling hand I see !
Each blessing to my soul more dear,
Because conferred by thee.

In every joy that crowns my days,
In every pain I bear,
My heart shall find delight in praise,
Or seek relief in prayer.

When gladness wings my favored hour,
Thy love my thoughts shall fill ;
Resigned, when storms of sorrow lower,
My soul shall meet thy will.

My lifted eye, without a tear,
  The gathering storm shall see;
My steadfast heart shall know no fear;
  That heart shall rest on thee.

57.   8s, 7s & 4s.

GUIDE me, O thou great Jehovah!
  Pilgrim through this barren land;
I am weak, but thou art mighty,
  Hold me with thy powerful hand:
    Bread of heaven!
Feed me now and evermore.

Open now the crystal fountain,
  Whence the healing waters flow;
Let the fiery, cloudy pillar
  Lead me all my journey through:
    Strong Deliverer,
Be thou still my strength and shield.

When I tread the verge of Jordan,
  Bid my anxious fears subside:
Thou of death and hell the conqueror,
  Land me safe on Canaan's side;
    Songs of praises
I will ever give to thee.

58.   C. M.

O FOR a faith that will not shrink,
  Though pressed by every foe,
That will not tremble on the brink
  Of any earthly woe

That will not murmur nor complain
  Beneath the chastening rod,
But. in the hour of grief or pain,
  Will lean upon its God.

A faith that shines more bright and clear
  When tempests rage without;
That when in danger knows no fear,
  In darkness feels no doubt.

Lord, give us such a faith as this,
  And then whate'er may come,
We'll taste, e'en here, the hallowed bliss
  Of an eternal home.

59. C. M.

GOD works in a mysterious way,
  His wonders to perform;
He plants his footsteps in the sea
  And rides upon the storm.

Ye fearful saints, fresh courage take,
  The clouds ye so much dread,
Are big with mercy, and shall break
  In blessings on your head.

Judge not the Lord by feeble sense,
  But trust him for his grace;
Behind a frowning Providence
  He hides a smiling face.

His purposes will ripen fast,
  Unfolding every hour;
The bud may have a bitter taste,
  But sweet will be the flower.

60.   7s.

JESUS, lover of my soul,
    Let me to thy bosom fly,
While the raging billows roll,
    While the tempest still is high.

Hide me, O my Saviour! hide,
    Till the storm of life is past;
Safe into the haven guide,
    O receive my soul at last!

Other refuge have I none;
    Hangs my helpless soul on thee:
Leave, O leave me not alone!
    Still support and comfort me.

All my trust on thee is stayed;
    All my help from thee I bring:
Cover my defenseless head
    With the shadow of thy wing.

61.   11s.

THOUGH troubles assail, and dangers af-
    fright;
Though friends should all fail, and foes all unite:
Yet one thing secures us, whatever betide;
The promise assures us, the Lord will provide.

The birds, without barn or storehouse, are fed;
From them let us learn to trust for our bread;
His saints what is fitting shall ne'er be denied,
So long as 'tis written, the Lord will provide.

No strength of our own, nor goodness we claim;
Our trust is all thrown on Jesus' name:
In this our strong tower for safety we hide;
The Lord is our power, the Lord will provide.

Union with Christ.

62.   C. M.

THE glorious universe around,
  The heavens with all their train,
Sun, moon, and stars, are firmly bound
  In one mysterious chain.

The earth, the ocean, and the sky,
  To form one world agree;
Where all that walk, or swim, or fly,
  Compose one family.

God in creation thus displays
  His wisdom and his might,
While all his works with all his ways
  Harmoniously unite.

In one fraternal bond of love,
  One fellowship of mind,
The saints below and saints above
  Their bliss and glory find.

Oh! may our union form a part
  Of that thrice happy whole;
Derive its pulse from Christ, the heart,
  Its life from Christ, the soul.

63.   S. M.

LET party names no more
    The Christian world o'erspread;
Gentile and Jew, and bond and free,
    Are one in Christ, their Head.

Among the saints on earth
    Let mutual love be found;
Heirs of the same inheritance,
    With mutual blessings crowned.

Thus will the Church below
    Resemble that above—
Where streams of pleasure ever flow,
    And every heart is love.

64.   7s.

CHRIST, from whom all blessings flow,
    Perfecting the saints below,
Hear us, who thy nature share,—
Who thy mystic body are,
Join us, in one Spirit join;
Let us still receive of thine;
Still for more on thee we call,
Thou who fillest all in all.

Sweetly may we all agree,
Touch'd with softest sympathy;
Kindly for each other care;
Every member feel its share.
Many are we now and one;
We who Jesus hath put on:
Names, and sects, and parties fall:
Thou, O Christ, art all in all.

65. L. M.

SAVIOUR of peace and unity,
 Send down thy mild pacific Dove;
We all shall then in one agree,
 And breathe the spirit of thy love.

We all shall think and speak the same
 Delightful lesson of thy grace:
One undivided Christ proclaim,
 And jointly glory in thy praise.

O let us take a softer mould,
 Blended and gather'd into thee;
Under one Shepherd make one fold,
 Where all is love and harmony.

So shall the world believe and know
 That God hath sent thee from above,
When thou art seen in us below,
 And every soul displays thy love.

66. C. M.

OUR God is love; and all his saints
 His image bear below:
The heart with love to God inspired,
 With love to man will glow.

None who are truly born of God
 Can live in enmity;
Then may we love each other, Lord,
 As we are loved by thee.

So may the unbelieving world
 See how true Christians love;
And glorify our Saviour's grace,
 And seek that grace to prove.

67. S. M.

BLEST be the tie that binds
Our hearts in Christian love:
The fellowship of kindred minds
Is like to that above.

Before our Father's throne
We pour our ardent prayers;
Our fears, our hopes, our aims are one—
Our comforts and our cares.

We share our mutual woes;
Our mutual burdens bear;
And often for each other flows
The sympathizing tear.

We're one in Christ our Head;
In him we grow and thrive:
He is our ever-living Head;
Our hopes in him revive.

68. C. M.

LO! what an entertaining sight
Those friendly brethren prove,
Whose cheerful hearts and hands unite
In labor and in love!

Where streams of life, from Christ the spring,
Descend to every soul;
And heavenly peace, with balmy wing,
Shades and bedews the whole.

'Tis pleasant as the morning dews
That fall on Zion's hill,
Where God his mildest glory shows,
And makes his grace distill.

69. H. M.

WHY hast thou cast our lot
  In the same age and place .
And why together brought
  To see each other's face ;—
To join with softest sympathy,
And fiix our friendly souls in thee ?

Didst thou not make us one,
  That we might one remain ;—
Together travel on,
  And bear each other's pain ;—
Till all thy utmost goodness prove,
And rise renew'd in perfect love ?

Surely thou didst unite
  Our kindred spirits here,
That all hereafter might
  Before thy Throne appear ;—
Meet at the marriage of the Lamb,
And all thy gracious love proclaim.

70 C. M.

LIFT up your hearts to things above,
  Ye followers of the Lamb,
And join with us to praise his love,
  And glorify his name.

We for his sake count all things loss ;
  On earthly good look down ;
And joyfully sustain the cross,
  Till we receive the crown.

O let us stir each other up,
  Our faith by works to approve,—
By holy, purifying hope,
  And the sweet task of love.

UNION

71.   C. M.

SAVIOUR, look down with pitying eyes;
  Our jarring wills control;
Le' cordial, kind affections rise,
  And harmonize the soul.

Rebuke our rage; our passions chide;
  Our stubborn wills control;
Beat down our wrath, root out our pride
  And calm each troubled soul.

Subdue in us the carnal mind;
  Its enmity destroy;
With cords of love our spirits bind,
  And melt us into joy.

Us into closest union draw,
  And in our inward parts
Let kindness sweetly write her law,
  And love command our hearts.

72.   C. M.

HOW pleasant thus to dwell below,
  In fellowship of love;
And though we part, 'tis bliss to know
  The good shall meet above.

Yes, happy thought! when we are free
  From earthly grief and pain,
In Heaven we shall each other see,
  And never part again.

Then let us each, in strength Divine,
  Still walk in wisdom's ways;
That we, with those we love, may join
  In never ending praise.

73.   C. M.

HELP us to help each other, Lord;
　　Each other's cross to bear:
Let each his friendly aid afford,
　　And feel his brother's care.

Help us to bear each other up;
　　Our little stock improve;
Increase our faith, confirm our hopes
　　And perfect us in love.

Up into thee, our living Head,
　　Let us in all things grow,
Till thou hast made us free indeed,
　　And Christ-like here below.

74.   C. M.

HOW sweet, how heavenly is the sight,
　　When those who love the Lord
In one another's peace delight,
　　And so fulfill his Word.

When, free from envy, scorn and pride,
　　Our wishes all above,
Each can his brother's failings hide,
　　And show a brother's love!

Let love, in one delightful stream,
　　Through every bosom flow;
And union sweet, and dear esteem,
　　In every action glow.

Love is the golden chain that binds
　　The happy souls above;
And he's an heir of Heaven, who finds
　　His bosom glow with love.

75. S. M.

BLEST are the sons of peace,
  Whose hearts and hopes are one;
Whose kind designs to serve and please
  Through all their actions run.

Blest is the pious house
  Where zeal and friendship meet;
Their songs of praise, their mingled vows,
  Make their communion sweet.

76. L. M.

COME, Christian brethren! ere we part,
  Join every voice and every heart,
One solemn hymn to God we raise,
One final song of grateful praise.

Christians! we here may meet no more,
But there is yet a happier shore;
And there, releas'd from toil and pain,
Dear brethren, we shall meet again.

77. 8s & 7s.

MAY the grace of Christ, our Saviour,
  And the Father's boundless love,
With the Holy Spirit's favor,
  Rest upon us from above.

Thus may we abide in union
  With each other and the Lord,
And possess, in sweet communion,
  Joys which earth can not afford.

Our Nation for Christ

---

78.   6s & 4s.

MY country, 'tis of thee,
  Sweet land of liberty,
    Of thee I sing.
Land where my fathers died,
Land of the pilgrim's pride,
From every mountain side
    Let freedom ring.

My native country, thee—
Land of the noble, free—
    Thy name—I love;
I love thy rocks and rills,
Thy woods and templed hills;
My heart with rapture thrills
    Like that above.

Let music swell the breeze,
And ring from all the trees
    Sweet freedom's song;

Let mortal tongues awake ;
Let all that breathe partake ;
Let rocks their silence break—
  The sound prolong.

Our fathers' God, to thee,
Author of liberty,
    To thee we sing :
Long may our land be bright
With freedom's holy light ;
Protect us by thy might,
    Great God, our King.

79.   8s & 7s.

WE come, we come, a joyful band,
    As patriots of the nation :
We're join'd in heart, we're join'd in hand,
  To keep the Constitution !

We come, we come, with joyful eyes ;
  We fear no usurpation :
Our fathers fought to win the prize,
  And keep the Constitution !

We come, we come—'tis Freedom's cause
  Excites our admiration :
Columbia's sons maintain her laws,
  And keep the Constitution !

We come, we come, our God to praise
  For our exalted station ;
To thank him for such happy days,
  And keep the Constitution.

80.   L. M.

GREAT God of nations, now to thee
   Our hymn of gratitude we raise;
With humble heart and bending knee,
   We offer thee our song of praise.

Thy name we bless, Almighty God,
   For all the kindness thou hast shown
To this fair land the pilgrims trod,—
   This land we fondly call our own.

Great God, preserve us in thy fear;
   In danger still our guardian be;
O, spread thy truth's bright precepts here,
   Let all the people worship thee.

81.   6s & 4s.

GOD save our native land,
   A firm, united band,
     We pray, O Lord!
Saviour, reign over us;
Make us victorious,
Happy and glorious:
     God save our land!

The choicest gifts in store
On us be pleas'd to pour,
     O God, our King!
Defend our land and laws,
And ever give us cause
To praise, with heart and voice,
     Jesus our King.

82.   10s & 11s.

O! SAY, can you see by the dawn's early
light,
  What so proudly we hailed at the twilight's
    last gleaming,
Whose stripes and bright stars through the peril-
  ous fight,
  O'er the ramparts we watched, were so gal-
    lantly streaming;
And the rocket's red glare, the bombs bursting
  in air,
  Gave proof through the night that our flag
    was still there;

CHORUS.

  O! say, does the star-spangled banner still
    wave
  O'er the land of the free and the home of the
    brave?

O! thus be it ever when freemen shall stand
  Between their loved home and the war's deso-
    lation;
Bless'd with victory and peace, may the Heaven-
  rescued land
  Praise the Power that hath made and pre-
    served us a nation!
Then conquer we must, when our cause it is
  just,
  And this be our motto, "In God is our trust!"

CHORUS.

  And the star-spangled banner in triumph shall
    wave
  O'er the land of the free and the home of the
    brave.

83. 7s & 6s.

WE came with hearts of gladness
 To breathe our songs of praise,
Let not a note of sadness
 Be blended in our lays;
For 'tis a hallow'd story,
 The theme of Freedom's birth:
Our fathers' deeds of glory
 Are echoed round the earth.

Soon Freedom's loud hosannas
 Shall burst from every voice,
And mountains and savannas
 Roll back the sound—rejoice!
Then raise the song of Freedom—
 The loudest, sweetest lay;
The captive's chains are riven,
 And Liberty shall reign.

84. 6s & 4s.

GOD bless our native land!
 Firm may she ever stand
  Through storm and night!
When the wild tempests rave,
Ruler of winds and wave!
Do thou our country save,
  By thy great might.

For her our prayer shall rise
To God above the skies;
  On him we call:
Thou who hast heard each sigh,
Watching each weeping eye,
Be thou forever nigh:
  God save us all.

85. L. M.

OUR flag is there, our flag is there,
  We'll greet it with three loud huzzas;
Our flag is there, our flag is there,
  Behold the glorious stripes and stars.
Stout hearts have fought for that bright flag,
  Strong hands sustained it mast-head high,
And Oh! to see how proud it waves,
  Brings tears of joy to every eye.

That flag has stood the battle's roar,
  With foemen stout, with foemen brave;
Strong hands have sought that flag to lower,
  And found a sure and speedy grave.
That flag is known on every shore,
  The standard of a gallant band,
Alike unstained in peace and war,
  It floats o'er freedom's happy land

86. P. M.

OPPRESSION shall not always reign,
  There dawns a brighter day,
When freedom, burst from every chain,
  Shall have triumphant sway.

Then right shall over might prevail,
  And truth, like hero armed in mail,
The hosts of tyrant wrong assail,
  And hold eternal sway.

The hour of triumph comes apace,
  The sure and promised hour,
When earth upon a ransomed race
  Her beauteous gifts shall shower.

Ring, Liberty, thy glorious bell!
Bid high thy sacred banner swell!
Let trump on trump, the triumph tell
Of heaven's redeeming power.

87.   8s & 9s.

THE angels of freedom are calling,
    Their music is borne from the sky;
The chains of the bondsmen are falling;
    The jubilee morning is nigh.
Now chant ye the mighty evangel,
    And hasten the spirit to free;
For liberty's beautiful angel
    Hath come from the Father to thee.

The stars in their glory are singing—
    The race of oppression is run;
For slaves into heroes are springing,
    And love binds all nations in one.
Christ comes in the liberty-angel;
    He hastens the spirit to free,
And speaks through the holy evangel,
    That comes from the Father to thee.

88.   P. M.

BEAUTIFUL flag! our country's pride,
    Long may thy Stars and Stripes float wide,
Over land and over sea;
Beautiful flag of the noble free!
Beautiful flag of the noble free!
    Beautiful flag, beautiful flag,
    Flag of the nation, beautiful, beautiful flag.

Glorious flag! no traitor's hand,
Ere shall pluck thee from our land,
    Never while God's our hope and trust,

Shall the flag of our country lay in dust!
Shall the flag of our country lay in dust!
　　Beautiful, &c.

Float on, float on, o'er fort and tower,
Glorious in thy silent power,
　Every living freeman holds
　A share in the wave of thy silken folds!
　A share in the wave of thy silken folds!
　　Beautiful, &c.

89.　　7s & 8s.

HAIL! Columbia, happy land,
　Hail! ye heroes, heaven-born band,
Who fought and bled in Freedom's cause;
Who fought and bled in Freedom's cause,
And when the storm of war was gone
Enjoy'd the peace your valor won:
Let Independence be your boast;
Ever mindful what it cost,
Ever grateful for the prize,
Let its altar reach the skies.
　　Firm, united let us be,
　　Rallying round our liberty:
　　As a band of brothers joined,
　　Peace and safety we shall find.

Sound, sound the trump of fame!
Let Washington's great name
Ring thro' the world with loud applause,
Ring thro' the world with loud applause;
Let every clime, to Freedom dear,
Listen with a joyful ear:
With equal skill, with godlike power,
He governs in the fearful hour
Of horrid war, or guides with ease
The happier times of honest peace.
　　Firm, united, &c

At Home with Christ.

90.   11s.

'MID scenes of confusion and creature com-
    plaints,
How sweet to my soul is communion with saints;
To find at the banquet of mercy there's room,
And feel in the presence of Jesus at home.
       Home, home; sweet, sweet home;
       Prepare me, dear Saviour, for
                Heaven, my home.

Sweet bonds that unite all the children of peace!
And thrice precious Jesus, whose love cannot
    cease!
Though oft from thy presence in sadness I roam,
I long to behold thee in glory at home.
       Home, home, &c.

While here in the valley of conflict I stay,
Oh, give me submission and strength as my day;
In all my afflictions to thee would I come,
Rejoicing in hope of my glorious home.
       Home, home, &c.

91.   8s & 4s.

WHEN for eternal worlds we steer,
    And seas are calm and skies are clear,
And faith in lively exercise,
And distant hills of Canaan rise,
The soul for joy then claps her wings,
And loud her lovely sonnet sings,
                Vain world—adieu!

The nearer that she draws to land,
More eager all her powers expand;
With steady helm and free-bent sail,
Her anchor drops within the veil;
Again for joy she claps her wings,
And her celestial sonnet sings,
              With Christ—at home.

92.   P. M.

I'M a pilgrim, and I'm a stranger;
    I can tarry, I can tarry but a night.
Do not detain me, for I'm going
To where the fountains are ever flowing.
           I'm a pilgrim, &c.

There the glory is ever shining:
I am longing, I am longing for the sight.
Here in this country, so dark and dreary,
I have been wandering forlorn and weary.
           I'm a pilgrim, &c.

There's the city to which I journey;
My Redeemer, my Redeemer is its light:
There is no sorrow, nor any sighing,
There is no sin there, nor any dying.
           I'm a pilgrim, &c.

93.   7s.

VITAL spark of heavenly flame !
    Quit, O quit this mortal frame !
Trembling, hoping, lingering, flying,
O the pain, the bliss of dying !
Cease fond nature, cease thy strife,
And let me languish into life !

Hark ! they whisper ! angels say,
"Sister spirit come away !"
What is this absorbs me quite,
Steals my spirits, draws my breath ?
Tell me, my soul, can this be death ?

The world recedes ! it disappears ;
Heaven opens on my eyes ! my ears
With sounds seraphic ring :
Lend, lend your wings ! I mount, I fly !
O grave ! where is thy victory ?
O death ! where is thy sting ?

94.   8s 7s & 5s.

IN the Christian's home in glory
    There remains a land of rest ;
There my Saviour's gone before me,
    To fulfill my soul's request.

CHORUS.

There is rest for the weary,
There is rest for the weary,
There is rest for the weary,
    There is rest for you—
On the other side of Jordan,
In the sweet fields of Eden,
Where the tree of life is blooming,
    There is rest for you.

He is fitting up my mansion,
  Which eternally shall stand,
For my stay shall not be transient
  In that holy, happy land.

Sing, O sing, ye heirs of glory;
  Shout your triumphs as you go:
Zion's gates will open for you,
  You shall find an entrance thro'.

95.   8s & 7s.

MY days are gliding swiftly by,
  And I a pilgrim stranger,
Would not detain them as they fly,
  Those hours of toil and danger.

CHORUS.

For oh! we stand on Jordan's strand,
  Our friends are passing over,
And, just before, the shining shore
  We may almost discover.

We'll gird our loins, my brethren dear,
  Our heavenly home discerning;
Our absent Lord has left us word,
  Let every lamp be burning.

Should coming days be cold and dark,
  We need not cease our singing;
That perfect rest naught can molest,
  Where golden harps are ringing.

Let sorrow's rudest tempest blow,
  Each chord on earth to sever;
Our King says come, and there's our home,
  Forever, oh! forever!

96.　11s.

I WOULD not live alway: I ask not to stay
　Where storm after storm rises dark o'er the
　　way;
The few lurid mornings that dawn on us here
Are enough for life's woes, full enough for its
　　cheer.

I would not live alway; no—welcome the tomb;
Since Jesus has lain there, I dread not its gloom;
There, sweet be my rest, till he bid me ise,
To hail him in triumph ascending the skies.

Where the saints of all ages in harmony meet,
Their Saviour and brethren transported to greet
While the anthems of rapture unceasingly roll,
And the smile of Jesus is the feast of the soul ?

97.　C. M.

AROUND the throne of God in heaven
　Thousands of children stand,
Children whose sins are all forgiven,
　A holy, happy band.
　　　　Singing glory, glory,
　　　　Glory be to God on high.

In flowing robes of spotless white,
　See every one array'd,
Dwelling in everlasting light,
　And joys that never fade.
　　　　　　Singing, &c.

What brought them to that world above,
　That heaven so bright and fair,

Where all is peace and joy and love ?
How came those children there ?
Singing, &c.

Because the Saviour shed his blood
To wash away their sin ;
Bathed in that pure and precious flood,
Behold them white and clean !
Singing, &c.

On earth they sought the Saviour's grace,
On earth they loved his name ;
So now they see his blessed face,
And stand before the Lamb.
Singing, &c.

98.   10s.

JOYFULLY, joyfully, onward we move,
Bound to the land of bright spirits above ;
Jesus, our Saviour, in mercy says, Come,
Joyfully, joyfully haste to your home.
Soon will our pilgrimage end here below,
Soon to the presence of God we shall go ;
Then, if to Jesus our hearts have been given,
Joyfully, joyfully rest we in heaven.

Death with his arrow may soon lay us low,
Safe in our Saviour we fear not the blow ;
Jesus hath broken the bars of the tomb,
Joyfully, joyfully will we go home.
Bright will the morn of eternity dawn—
Death shall be conquer'd, his sceptre be gone:
Over the plains of sweet Canaan we'll roam,
Joyfully, joyfully, safely at home.

99.   8s.

BEAUTIFUL Zion, built above,
  Beautiful city, that I love,
Beautiful gates of pearly white,
Beautiful temple—God its light!
He who was slain on Calvary
Opens those pearly gates to me.

Beautiful heaven, where all is light,
Beautiful angels, clothed in white,
Beautiful strains, that never tire,
Beautiful harps through all the choir!
There shall I join the chorus sweet,
Worshipping at the Saviour's feet.

Beautiful crowns on every brow,
Beautiful palms the conquerors show,
Beautiful robes the ransom'd wear,
Beautiful all who enter there!
Thither I press with eager feet;
There shall my rest be long and sweet.

Beautiful throne for Christ, our King,
Beautiful songs the angels sing,
Beautiful rest, all wanderings cease,
Beautiful home of perfect peace!
There shall my eyes the Saviour see:
Haste to this heavenly home with me.

AT HOME.

100.   10s & 4s.

OUT on an ocean all boundless we ride,
    We're homeward bound;
Toss'd on the waves of a rough, restless tide,
    We're homeward bound.
Far from the safe, quiet harbour we've rode,
Seeking our Saviour's celestial abode,
Promise of which on us each he bestow'd,
    We're homeward bound.

We'll tell the world, as we journey along,
    We're homeward bound;
Try to persuade them to enter our throng,
    We're homeward bound.
Come, trembling sinner, forlorn and oppress'd,
Join in our number, oh, come and he blest,
Journey with us to the mansions of rest,
    We're homeward bound.

Into the harbour of heaven now we glide,
    We're home at last;
Softly we drift on its bright silver tide,
    We're home at last;
Glory to God! all our dangers are o'er,
We stand secure on the glorified shore.
Glory to God! we will shout evermore,
    We're home at last.

OLD HUNDRED.

PRAISE God, from whom all blessings flow
    Praise him, all creatures here below;
Praise him above, ye heavenly host,
Praise Father, Son, and Holy Ghost.

www.ingramcontent.com/pod-product-compliance
Lightning Source LLC
Chambersburg PA
CBHW032045090426
42733CB00030B/706

*9 7 8 3 7 4 4 7 7 9 4 4 9 *